HAPPY
B-DAY
♥

To: JANETH

From: MARIOLA

2013

Published by Sellers Publishing, Inc.
Photography © 2013 Jane Burton &
Mark Taylor/Warren Photographic

Book design by Rita Sowins, Sowins Design

Compiled by Robin Haywood

Sellers Publishing, Inc.
161 John Roberts Road, South Portland, Maine 04106
Visit our Web site sellerspublishing.com
E-mail: rsp@rsvp.com

Credits p. 64

ISBN 13: 978-1-4162-0964-5

No portion of this book may be reproduced or transmitted in any form, or by any means, electronic or mechanical, including photographing, recording, or by any information and storage retrieval system, without written permission from the publisher.

10 9 8 7 6 5 4 3 2 1

Printed and bound in China

S♥ul Mates

"...you had me at hello"

SELLERS
PUBLISHING

"I love that you get cold when it's 71 degrees out. I love that it takes you an hour and a half to order a sandwich. I love that you get a little crinkle above your nose when you're looking at me like I'm nuts. I love that after I spend a day with you I can still smell your perfume on my clothes, and I love that you are the last person I want to talk to before I go to sleep at night."

♥ *When Harry Met Sally . . .* , 1989.
Harry Burns (BILLY CRYSTAL) to
Sally Albright (MEG RYAN)

"If you love someone, you say it, you say it right then, out loud, otherwise the moment just passes you by."

❤ *My Best Friend's Wedding*, 1997.
Michael O'Neal (Dermot Mulroney) to
Julianne Potter (Julia Roberts)

"... I've got a sneaky feeling you'll find that love actually is all around."

❤ *Love Actually, 2003.* Voice of the prime minister (HUGH GRANT) over opening credits.

Westley: "Hear this now: I will always come for you."

Buttercup: "But how can you be sure?"

Westley: "This is true love — you think this happens every day?"

♥ *The Princess Bride*, 1987.
Westley (CARY ELWES) to Buttercup (ROBIN WRIGHT)

"It is only in the mysterious equations of love that any logic or reasons can be found. I am only here tonight because of you. You are the reason I am. You are all my reasons."

♥ *A Beautiful Mind*, 2002. John Nash (Russell Crowe) to Alicia Nash (Jennifer Connelly)

"... my heart is, and always will be, yours."

♥ *Sense and Sensibility* (film), 1995. Edward Ferrars (HUGH GRANT) to Elinor Dashwood (EMMA THOMPSON)

"I wanna make you smile whenever you're sad. Carry you around when your arthritis is bad. All I wanna do is grow old with you. I'll get your medicine when your tummy aches. Build you a fire if the furnace breaks.

Oh it could be so nice, growin' old with you. I'll miss you, kiss you, give you my coat when you are cold. Need you, feed you, I'll even let you hold the remote control. So let me do the dishes in our kitchen sink. Put you to bed when you've had too much to drink. Oh I could be the man who grows old with you. I wanna grow old with you."

❤ *The Wedding Singer*, 1998. Robbie Hart (ADAM SANDLER) singing to Julia Sullivan (DREW BARRYMORE)

> *"Shut up, just shut up.*
> *You had me at 'hello.'"*

♥ *Jerry Maguire*, 1996. Dorothy Boyd
(Renée Zellweger) to Jerry Maguire (Tom Cruise)

"I'm not a smart man, but I know what love is."

♥ *Forrest Gump*, 1994. Forrest Gump (Tom Hanks) to Jenny Curran (Robin Wright)

"Well, it was a million tiny little things that, when you added them all up, it-it just meant that we were supposed to be together . . . and I knew it."

❤ *Sleepless in Seattle*, 1993. Sam Baldwin (TOM HANKS) on the phone with radio talk-show host, Dr. Marcia Fieldstone; Annie Reed (MEG RYAN) is listening while driving

"Loretta, I love you. Not-not like they told you love is, and I didn't know this either, but love don't make things nice — it ruins everything. It breaks your heart. It makes things a mess. We aren't here to make things perfect. The snowflakes are perfect. The stars are perfect. Not us. Not us! We are here to ruin ourselves and — and to break our hearts and love the wrong people and, and die. I mean, the storybooks are bulls##t. Now I want you to come upstairs with me and — and get in my bed!"

♥ *Moonstruck*, 1987. Ronny Cammareri (NICOLAS CAGE) to Loretta Castorini (CHER)

[*Charles comes running after Carrie*]

Charles: "Um, look. Sorry, sorry. Ah, I just, um, well, this is a really stupid question, um, ah, and … particularly in view of our recent shopping excursion, but, um, I just wondered if by any chance, I mean obviously not because I guess I've only slept with nine people, but-but I-I just wondered … ah. I really feel, um, ah, in short, to recap in a slightly clearer version, ah, the words of

David Cassidy in fact, um, while he was still with the Partridge Family, ah, "I think I love you," and ah, I-I just wondered, well, by any chance you wouldn't like to ... Um ... ah ... ah ... No, no, no, of course not ... Um, I'm an idiot, he's not ... Excellent, excellent, fantastic, ah, I was gonna say lovely to see you, sorry to disturb ... Better get on..."

Carrie: "That was very romantic."

Charles: "Well, I thought it over a lot, you know, I wanted to get it just right."

❤ *Four Weddings and a Funeral*, 1994.
Charles (HUGH GRANT) and Carrie (ANDIE MACDOWELL)

Anna: "Can I stay for a while?"
William: "You can stay forever."

♥ *Notting Hill*, 1999. Anna Scott (Julia Roberts) and William Thacker (Hugh Grant)

"We'll always have Paris."

♥ *Casablanca*, 1943. Rick Blaine (Humphrey Bogart) to Ilsa Laszlo (Ingrid Bergman)

Mark: "I like you, very much."

Bridget: "Ah, apart from the smoking and the drinking and the vulgar mother and the verbal diarrhea."

Mark: "No, I like you very much. Just as you are."

♥ *Bridget Jones's Diary*, 2001. Mark Darcy (COLIN FIRTH) and Bridget Jones (RENÉE ZELLWEGER)

Harry: "I've been doing a lot of thinking, and the thing is, I love you."

Sally: "What?"

Harry: "I love you."

Sally: "How do you expect me to respond to this?"

Harry: "How about, you love me too."

Sally: "How about, I'm leaving."

❤ *When Harry Met Sally . . .* , 1989. Harry Burns (BILLY CRYSTAL) and Sally Albright (MEG RYAN)

*"You can't hurt me.
Westley and I are joined by the bonds of love.
And you cannot track that,
not with a thousand bloodhounds,
and you cannot break it,
not with a thousand swords."*

❤ *The Princess Bride*, 1987. Buttercup (ROBIN WRIGHT) to Prince Humperdinck (CHRIS SARANDON)

"Look, I guarantee there'll be tough times. I guarantee that at some point, one or both of us is going to want to get out of this thing. But I also guarantee that if I don't ask you to be mine, I'll regret it for the rest of my life. Because I know in my heart you're the only one for me."

❤ *Runaway Bride*, 1999. Ike Graham (RICHARD GERE) to Maggie Carpenter (JULIA ROBERTS)

"I came here tonight because when you realize you want to spend the rest of your life with somebody, you want the rest of your life to start as soon as possible."

♥ *When Harry Met Sally . . .*, 1989. Harry Burns (BILLY CRYSTAL) to Sally Albright (MEG RYAN)

> "... I'm also just a girl,
> standing in front of a boy,
> asking him to love her."

❤ *Notting Hill*, 1999. Anna Scott (JULIA ROBERTS) to William Thacker (HUGH GRANT)

"You said you couldn't be with someone who didn't believe in you. Well, I believed in you. I just didn't believe in me. I love you . . . always."

❤ *Pretty in Pink*, 1986. Blane McDonnagh (ANDREW MCCARTHY) to Andie Walsh (MOLLY RINGWALD)

Ronny: "I'm in love with you."
Loretta: [*slaps him twice*] "Snap out of it!"

❤ *Moonstruck*, 1987.
Ronny Cammareri (NICOLAS CAGE)
and Loretta Castorini (CHER)

You should be kissed, and often,

❤ *Gone with the Wind*, 1939. Rhett Butler (Clark Gable) to Scarlett O'Hara (Vivien Leigh)

...and by someone who knows how."

"Love is too weak a word for what I feel — I luuurve you, you know, I loave you, I luff you, two f's, yes I have to invent, of course I do, don't you think I do?"

♥ *Annie Hall*, 1977. Alvy Singer (WOODY ALLEN) to Annie Hall (DIANE KEATON)

"It doesn't matter if the guy is perfect or the girl is perfect, as long as they are perfect for each other."

♥ *Good Will Hunting*, 1997.
Will Hunting (MATT DAMON)

Paul: "I love you."

Holly: "So what?"

Paul: "So what? So plenty! I love you, you belong to me!"

Holly: [*tearfully*] "No. People don't belong to people."

Paul: "Of course they do!"

Holly: "I'll never let anybody put me in a cage."

Paul: "I don't want to put you in a cage, I want to love you!"

❤ *Breakfast at Tiffany's*, 1961. Paul Varjak (GEORGE PEPPARD) and Holly Golightly (AUDREY HEPBURN)

"Sometimes in life there really are bonds formed that can never be broken. Sometimes you really can find that one person who will stand by you no matter what. Maybe you'll find it in a spouse and celebrate it with your dream wedding. But there's also the chance that the one person you can count on for a lifetime, the one person who knows you sometimes better than you know yourself, is the same person who's been standing beside you all along."

❤ *Bride Wars*, 2009. Marion St. Claire (CANDICE BERGEN)

"Take love, multiply it by infinity and take it to the depths of forever... And you still have only a glimpse of how I feel for you."

♥ *Meet Joe Black*, 1998. Joe Black (BRAD PITT) to Susan Parrish (CLAIRE FORLANI)

"It seems right now that all I've ever done in my li[fe]

♥ *The Bridges of Madison County*, 1995. Robert Kincaid (CLINT EASTWOOD) to Francesca Johnson (MERYL STREEP)

Sean: "Do you have a soul mate?"

Will: "Define that."

Sean: "Someone you can relate to, someone who opens things up for you."

Will: "Sure, I got plenty."

Sean: "Well, name them."

Will: "Shakespeare, Nietzsche, Frost, O'Conner …"

Sean: "Well that's great. They're all dead."

Will: "Not to me, they're not."

Sean: "You can't have a lot of dialogue with them."

Will: "Not without a heater and some serious smelling salts."

❤ *Good Will Hunting*, 1997. Will Hunting (MATT DAMON) and Sean Maguire (ROBIN WILLIAMS)

Credits

p. 5 *When Harry Met Sally . . .*, 1989. (Castle Rock Entertainment, Nelson Entertainment). Directed by Rob Reiner, screenplay by Nora Ephron

p. 7 *My Best Friend's Wedding*, 1997. (TriStar Pictures, Zucker Brothers Productions, Predawn Productions). Directed by P.J. Hogan, screenplay by Ronald Bass

p. 8 *Love Actually*, 2003. (Universal Pictures, Studio Canal, Working Title Films, DNA Films). Directed and written by Richard Curtis

p. 10 *The Princess Bride*, 1987. (Act III Communications, Buttercup Films Ltd, The Princess Bride Ltd). Directed by Rob Reiner, screenplay by William Goldman

p. 12 *A Beautiful Mind*, 2002. (Universal Pictures, DreamWorks SKG, Imagine Entertainment). Directed by Ron Howard, screenplay by Akiva Goldsman

p. 15 *Sense and Sensibility* (film), 1995. (Columbia Pictures, Mirage). Directed by Ang Lee, screenplay by Emma Thompson from a story by Jane Austen

p. 16 *The Wedding Singer*, 1998. (Juno Pix, New Line Cinema, Robert Simonds Productions). Directed by Frank Coraci, screenplay by Tim Herlihy

p. 18 *Jerry Maguire*, 1996. (TriStar Pictures, Gracie Films). Directed and written by Cameron Crowe

p. 21 *Forrest Gump*, 1994. (Paramount Pictures). Directed by Robert Zemeckis, screenplay by Eric Roth

p. 23 *Sleepless in Seattle*, 1993. (TriStar Pictures). Directed by Nora Ephron and co-written by Nora Ephron, Jeff Arch, and David S. Ward, from a story by Jeff Arch

p. 24 *Moonstruck*, 1987. (Metro-Goldwyn-Mayer, Star Partners). Directed by Norman Jewison, screenplay by John Patrick Shanley

pp 26 *Four Weddings and a Funeral*, 1994. (PolyGram Filmed Entertainment, Channel Four Films, Working Title Films). Directed by Mike Newell, screenplay by Richard Curtis

p. 28 *Notting Hill*, 1999. (PolyGram Filmed Entertainment, Title Films. Bookshop Productions, Notting Hill Pictures). Directed by Roger Michell, screenplay by Richard Curtis

p. 31 *Casablanca*, 1942. (Warner Bros.). Directed by Michael Curtiz, screenplay by Julius E. Epstein, Howard E. Koch, and Philip G. Epstein

p. 32 *Bridget Jones's Diary*, 2001. (Miramax Films, Universal Pictures, Studio Canal, Working Title Films, Little Bird). Directed by Sharon Maguire, screenplay by Andrew Davies, Helen Fielding, and Richard Curtis

p. 34 *When Harry Met Sally . . .*, 1989. (Castle Rock Entertainment, Nelson Entertainment). Directed by Rob Reiner, screenplay by Nora Ephron

p. 37 *The Princess Bride*, 1987. (Act III Communications, Buttercup Films Ltd, The Princess Bride Ltd). Directed by Rob Reiner, screenplay by William Goldman

p. 39 *Runaway Bride*, 1999. (Paramount Pictures, Touchstone Pictures, Interscope Communications, Lakeshore Entertainment). Directed by Garry Marshall, screenplay by Sara Parriott and Josann McGibbon

p. 40 *When Harry Met Sally . . .*, 1989. (Castle Rock Entertainment, Nelson Entertainment). Directed by Rob Reiner, screenplay by Nora Ephron

p. 42 *Notting Hill*, 1999. (PolyGram Filmed Entertainment, Title Films. Bookshop Productions, Notting Hill Pictures). Directed by Roger Michell, screenplay by Richard Curtis

p. 44 *Pretty in Pink*, 1986. (Paramount Pictures). Directed by Howard Deutch, screenplay by John Hughes

p. 46 *Moonstruck*, 1987. (Metro-Goldwyn-Mayer, Star Partners). Directed by Norman Jewison, screenplay by John Patrick Shanley

p. 48 *Gone with the Wind*, 1939. (Selznick International Pictures, Metro-Goldwyn-Mayer). Directed by George Cukor, Victor Fleming, and Sam Wood; screenplay by Sidney Howard, Oliver H.P. Garrett, Ben Hecht, John William Van Druten, and Jo Swerling; from a story by Margaret Mitchell

p. 50 *Annie Hall*, 1977. (Rollins-Jaffe Productions). Directed by Woody Allen, screenplay by Woody Allen and Marshall Brickman

p. 53 *Good Will Hunting*, 1997. (Be Gentlemen Limited Partnership, Lawrence Bender Productions, Miramax Films). Directed by Gus Van Sant, screenplay by Matt Damon and Ben Affleck

p. 54 *Breakfast at Tiffany's*, 1961. (Jurow-Shepherd). Directed by Blake Edwards, screenplay by George Axelrod; from a novel by Truman Capote

p. 57 *Bride Wars*, 2009. (Fox 2000 Pictures, Regency Enterprises, New Regency Pictures, Firm Films, Dune Entertainment, Sunrise Entertainment (II). Directed by Gary Winick, screenplay by Casey Rose Wilson, Greg DePaul, and June Diane Raphael

p. 59 *Meet Joe Black*, 1998. (Universal Pictures, City Light Films). Directed by Martin Brest, screenplay by Jeff Reno, Ron Osborn, Kevin Wade and Bo Goldman; from a story by Gladys Lehman, Maxwell Anderson, Alberto Casella, and Walter Ferris

p. 60 *The Bridges of Madison County*, 1995. (Warner Bros., Amblin Entertainment, Malpaso Productions). Directed by Clint Eastwood, screenplay by Richard LaGravenese; from a story by Robert James Waller

p. 62 *Good Will Hunting*, 1997. (Be Gentlemen Limited Partnership, Lawrence Bender Productions, Miramax Films). Directed by Gus Van Sant, screenplay by Matt Damon and Ben Affleck